WINTER LIGHT
A SOJOURNER'S 40 DAY JOURNAL

ERIC KAMPMANN

**BEAUFORT
BOOKS**

For inquiries about volume orders, please contact:
Beaufort Books27 West 20th Street, Suite 1103
New York, NY 10011sales@beaufortbooks.com

Published in the United States by Beaufort Books www.beaufortbooks.com

Distributed by Midpoint Trade Books,
a division of Independent Book Publishers

www.midpointtrade.com
www.ipgbook.com

Interior design by Neuwirth & Associates, Inc.
Cover design by Mark Karis
Cover photo by Eric Kampmann

Library of Congress Data on file

Paperback: 9780825309892
Ebook: 9780825308680

Printed in The United States

"Thus says the LORD: 'Stand by the roads, and look, and ask for the ancient paths, where the good way is; and walk in it, and find rest for your souls. But they said, "We will not walk in it."'"

—JEREMIAH 6 : 16

"The safest road to hell is the gradual one—the gentle slope, soft underfoot, without sudden turnings, without milestones, without signposts."

—C. S. LEWIS

PREFACE

The heart of a man plans his way,
but the LORD establishes his steps.

—PROVERBS 16:9

John Eldredge in his short book *Epic* uses this as his subtitle: "The Story God is Telling and the Role that is Yours to Play." In the first chapter Eldredge quotes Sam, the Hobbit, in *The Lord of the Rings* asking, "I wonder what sort of tale we've fallen into?" Eldredge goes on to say, "Sam assumes that there is a story; there is something larger going on. He also assumes that they have tumbled into it, been swept up into it." Before 1987, I would not have believed that I was in any story but my own. But in the spring of that year my whole concept of story would be turned on its head.

As a young boy, I thought Manhattan was the center of everything that was romantic and mysterious. I would occasionally travel to the city with my father by train and would come away with the conviction that New York was my city and that I would someday move there.

My attraction to the great city would later take on a literary cast. As I grew older, New York became for me the city of Melville, Whitman and Fitzgerald, a never ceasing engine of dreams and money, drawing people from around the world to live and work in the steel and glass canyons that tower above the churning streets. F. Scott Fitzgerald particularly influenced my thinking as when in *The Great Gatsby* he describes the experience of approaching the city from afar:

"Over the great bridge, with the sunlight through the girders making a constant flicker upon the moving cars, with the city rising up across the river in white heaps and sugar lumps all built with a wish out of non-olfactory money. The city seen from the Queensboro Bridge is always the city seen for the first time, in its first wild promise of all the mystery and beauty in the world."

In September 1969, I was married in New York City and soon secured a job as a sales rep for a book publisher. Ten years later, I was vice president, director of sales at a major publishing house. In 1981,

I left that job to launch my own start up, but by 1987, I realized my company was in trouble and was skidding off the side of the road and then....

And then, one spring day I took an unscheduled detour by entering a church on Park Avenue. I was alone and the church was empty. Silence hung over the vast space and instead of turning back to rejoin the flood of people going somewhere in a hurry, I sat down. I had entered the church on an impulse and then I said a prayer on an impulse. I did not expect anything to happen one way or the other and soon enough I reemerged into the light and the flowing stream of seemingly determined people passing by.

Two weeks later, an angel must have entered my office because I received a very explicit message to get up, leave the building, find a bookstore and buy a Bible. Amazingly, I did just that: I found a bookstore a few blocks away and bought a beautifully made leather-bound Bible. And with that one act, everything in my life would begin to change.

In 1989, my company did declare Chapter 11. It should have disappeared forever at that point, but it emerged in 1991 from bankruptcy. Real miracles happened during this period. It was also in 1991 that I discovered a lectionary that gave me an excellent roadmap in my new quest to know the Old and New Testaments. Using the lectionary, I immersed myself in daily reading year after year. I also began to attend church, participate in Bible studies, listen to tapes and read as much as I could to supplement my daily biblical readings.

By 2001, I began compiling passages from the wisdom books in the Old Testament for my children mostly, but for other purposes as well. Those passages became a book I would call Tree of Life. Once the book was finished, I began to write short commentaries for each of the 365 wisdom passages chosen for the book.

By the end of the first full year of writing, I realized I wasn't ready for prime time, to put it mildly. I returned to the keyboard and for the next two years I rewrote and rewrote until I became confident in what was being said and how it was being said.

The first version of this book was published in 2008 and was called *Trail Thoughts*. In 2011, the book was reissued as *Signposts* and became the basis for a series of 365 daily podcasts with Senior Pastor Chuck Davis of Stanwich Church.

While in Israel in 2012, Chuck Davis and I committed to embarking on a new series of daily podcasts on Jesus as He is revealed to us in the four Gospels. After those were completed, I decided to write a new book based on the content of the podcasts. That book, *Getting to Know Jesus*, was published in 2016.

Finally, in November 2017, I started posting a psalm and a short commentary on Twitter and Facebook. In addition to the psalm, I included a photograph as a way of adding a new dimension to the experience of being in the Word of God daily.

What began as a short prayer in an empty church in Manhattan in 1987 had, unexpectedly, grown into a trilogy of devotionals that has put me in the middle of a story that I never expected to be in. At that time, I would have been incapable of thinking I was in any story but my own. But as I came to know the Bible, I began to see the larger narrative Eldredge writes about; I began to see that when I prayed to God for help that day in 1987, I opened a way through a door that revealed to me that I was being invited into a story that has been unfolding since the beginning.

CITY OF GOD

The LORD brought me forth as the first of his works,
before his deeds of old; I was appointed from eternity, from the
beginning, before the world began. When there were no oceans, I
was given birth, when there were no springs abounding with
water; before the mountains were settled in place, before the
hills, I was given birth, before he made the earth or its fields
or any of the dust of the world.

—PROVERBS 8:22–26

BEFORE THE CREATION OF THE WORLD

TODAY MANY ARE taught that life begins at birth and ends with the finality of death; they are taught that there is no reality to either God or to eternal life. The Bible, however, tells another story. According to Scripture, you and I were created by God before we were born. And from the beginning, He had a purpose for us.

Solomon tells us that God's wisdom was "appointed from eternity, from the beginning before the world began." This spiritual truth is echoed throughout the Bible. From David: "When I was woven together in the depths of the earth, your eyes saw my unformed body" (Psalm 139:15–16). From Jeremiah: "Before I formed you in the womb, I knew you; before you were born I set you apart" (Jeremiah 1:5). From Isaiah: "Before I was born the LORD called me, from my birth he has made mention of my name" (Isaiah 49:1). From Paul: "For he chose us in him before the creation of the world" (Ephesians 1:4). And Jesus says this at the end of His prayer for all believers: "Father, I want those you have given me to be with me where I am, and to see my glory, the glory you have given me because you loved me before the creation of the world" (John 17:24).

In our thoughtlessness, we can choose to disregard the reality of the existence of God. We are free to choose to live without Him, but like everything else, that choice has profound implications.

The highest heavens belong to the LORD, but the earth he has given to man. It is not the dead who praise the LORD, those who go down to silence; it is we who extol the LORD, both now and forevermore. Praise the LORD.

—PSALM 115:16–18

RETURNING TO THE ORIGINAL STORY LINE

THE BIBLICAL ACCOUNT of the first man begins in a garden: "Now the LORD God had planted a garden in the east, in Eden, and there he put the man he had formed" (Genesis 2:8). The garden was designed to be a good place for man, a place he could enjoy and cultivate: "The LORD God took the man and put him in the Garden of Eden to work it and take care of it (Genesis 2:15)."

God planted all kinds of trees and brought beasts of the field for the man to name. And God created a companion for the man so that together the man and the woman would fulfill God's purposes for them. From the very beginning, God created the earth for man's dominion. It was only when the man and the woman defied God's one prohibition that a very different story began to unfold.

At the center of the new story is betrayal, for where there was harmony, now we find rebellion; where there was a home, now we find exile; and where there was abundance, now we find hard labor and travail.

The original story line was radically changed by one act of thoughtless defiance. The new story is the tale that culminates as a sacrificial act of love on a cross on a mound outside the gates of Jerusalem. At that moment, all men and women once again could enter the original story line that had its origin in Eden.

It was not by their sword that they won the land,
nor did their arm bring them victory; it was your right hand,
your arm, and the light of your face, for you loved them.

—PSALM 44:3

HISTORY

IN MOST CONTEMPORARY accounts of historical events, man plays the central role of hero or villain. In Winston Churchill's four-volume *History of the English Speaking Peoples*, for example, the real hero is the genius of the peoples of the British nation. It is essentially a progressive view of history and, therefore, modern because it tells a tale of greater and greater national triumphs. It is a wonderful story of kings and queens and leaders of all sorts carrying the growing empire forward to its ordained destiny of a saving civilization. Yet in a sense, Churchill's account is a surprisingly unsatisfying account because the hand of God is nowhere to be found.

The Bible is also a work of history with its own kings and queens, battles won and lost, civilizations rising and falling, warriors and cowards, saints and villains. But while earthly events are important to the unfolding story, the supernatural hand of God is everywhere from the first page through the last.

If we subscribe to the biblical account of history, then the importance of particular civilizations diminishes substantially, while the salvation of the individual soul becomes paramount. From the fall in the Garden of Eden to the resurrection of Jesus Christ and the bestowing of the Holy Spirit, it is a story that continues to unfold to this very moment through people just like you and me. This history becomes the revelation of God's compelling purpose, with each one of us as participants in His great narrative: "It was not by their sword that they won the land . . . it was your right hand, your arm, and the light of your face, for you loved them."

The path of the righteous is like the first gleam of dawn,
shining ever brighter till the full light of day.
But the way of the wicked is like deep darkness;
they do not know what makes them stumble.

—PROVERBS 4:18–19

THE LANGUAGE OF GOD PART 1

SOLOMON COMPARES "RIGHTEOUSNESS" to the first light of morning, and in contrast, he compares the deeds of the "wicked" to deep darkness. The light and dark imagery point to our relationship with God in a language that speaks to our spiritual longing for holiness.

The language of Scripture has beauty and truth embedded within its very core, and it is through the power of its language that it reveals the presence and the power of God. The Bible opens with God saying, "Let there be light" (Genesis 1:3). Before there was light, the universe was void and without life and form.

And here is how John describes the second creation story, the birth of God's one and only Son: "In him was life, and that life was the light of men. The light shines in the darkness, but the darkness has not understood it" (John 1:4–5).

And here is Jesus during His three-year ministry: "I am the light of the world. Whoever follows me will never walk in darkness, but will have the light of life" (John 8:12). John echoes this in his first letter: "God is light; in him there is no darkness at all" (1 John 1:5).

When reading Scripture, look for patterns of imagery within the written word, for within these patterns is revelation. The power of the language of Scripture is the presence of the Holy Spirit embedded in the language. This language transcends time and place, for the Holy Spirit speaks to the deepest longings of the human heart, which yearns to shuck the things that would harm and destroy and to recover the righteousness that comes from God.

The words of the wise are like goads, their collected sayings like firmly embedded nails—given by one Shepherd. Be warned, my son, of anything in addition to them. Of making many books there is no end, and much study wearies the body.

—ECCLESIASTES 12:11–12

THE LANGUAGE OF GOD PART 2

How DO WE become literate in the language of the spirit of God? What are the "right words" given by "one Shepherd"?

Jesus is that "one Shepherd," but when He spoke, He was often misunderstood because He spoke in the figurative language of the Holy Spirit. Nicodemus came to Jesus with a literal spirit and so was bewildered when Jesus told him, "I tell you the truth, no one can see the kingdom of God unless he is born again" (John 3:3). Likewise, the Samaritan woman is blinded at first by her ethnic literalism: "You are a Jew and I am a Samaritan woman. How can you ask me for a drink?" (John 4:9). But Jesus speaks of another kind of water that never fails and that wells "up to eternal life" (John 4:14).

Then Jesus speaks of a time when all barriers will be broken down and one language will be spoken: "Yet a time is coming and has now come when the true worshipers will worship the Father in spirit and truth, for they are the kind of worshipers the Father seeks. God is spirit, and His worshipers must worship in spirit and in truth" (John 4:23–24).

If we are trapped in a spiritual literalism, then we should pray that our Emmaus moment will come: "And beginning with Moses and all the Prophets, he explained to them what was said in all the Scriptures concerning himself. . . . Then their eyes were opened and they recognized him, and he disappeared from their sight. They asked each other, 'Were not our hearts burning within us while he talked with us on the road and opened the Scriptures to us?'" (Luke 24:27, 31–32).

O God, you are my God, earnestly I seek you;

my soul thirsts for you, my body longs for you,

in a dry and weary land where there is no water.

—PSALM 63:1

THE LANGUAGE OF GOD PART 3

EVERY ONE WHO finds himself lost in a "dry and weary land" will experience physical thirst. But what about the soul? Is the Psalmist speaking about our physical need for water only?

When Jesus was passing through the parched land of Samaria, He came upon a woman at a well near the town of Sychar. While resting there, He asked this woman for water. When she questioned Him, He begins to speak figuratively about a different kind of "living water" that will become "a spring of water welling up to eternal life" (John 4:14).

At first, the woman is confused, but soon she realizes to whom she is speaking and goes away to tell her townspeople to "come, see a man who told me everything I ever did. Could this be the Christ?" (John 4:29).

Jesus uses figurative language to reveal a spiritual truth that remains the same in all places and times. We need to satisfy the thirst of the heart with the living water of the Spirit that is freely offered by God to all who will ask to drink it. The language of this world cannot adequately express the spiritual truth behind Jesus' words, which is why he uses figurative speech when revealing a spiritual truth.

Paul, speaking about the power of the Holy Spirit, says, "The Spirit searches all things, even the deep things of God. . . . This is what we speak, not in words taught us by human wisdom but in words taught by the Spirit, expressing spiritual truths in spiritual words. The man without the Spirit does not accept the things that come from the Spirit of God, for they are foolishness to him, and he cannot understand them, because they are spiritually discerned" (1 Corinthians 2:10, 13–14).

Every word of God is flawless; he is a shield to those
who take refuge in him. Do not add to his words,
or he will rebuke you and prove you a liar.

—PROVERBS 30:5–6

DO NOT ADD . . . OR SUBTRACT

FOR THOSE WHO consider God optional, the words of the Bible mean very little. There are others, however, who seem to take the Word of God seriously but want to add to it or subtract from it for their own purposes. For example, Thomas Jefferson excised the miracles because his eighteenth-century sensibility was offended by the improbability of the supernatural.

At the other end of the spectrum are the high-octane embellishers who believe that the Bible needs to be added to in order to be relevant to modern readers.

Either way, the authority of the biblical witness of God's Word is placed in doubt. If the enemies of God can find a small thread to unravel, then they can proceed to cast doubt on the whole fabric of God's revelation. In speaking about God's law, Moses warned against altering any of it: "Do not add to what I command you and do not subtract from it, but keep the commands of the LORD your God that I give you" (Deuteronomy 4:2).

The truth is that we should approach the Word of God with humility; we should have the attitude of a thirsty sojourner who wishes to drink in every word that God has blessed us with through His Holy Scripture.

Praise the Lord from the earth . . .
Let them praise the name of the LORD,
for his name alone is exalted;
his splendor is above the earth and the heavens.

—PSALM 148:7,13

TEACH US TO PRAY

THE LORD, WHOSE "splendor is above the earth and the heavens," stooped to take us by the hand to teach us how to speak to Him in prayer. Jesus gave us the Lord's Prayer in His Sermon on the Mount, but He did not ask us to slavishly memorize it and repeat it by rote. He wanted it to come from a heart filled with love, devotion, and gratitude. He gave us the form of prayer to pray and asked each of His followers to fill it in with the words that come from the heart.

Paraphrasing Jesus, we might pray: *Father, holy is your name. I pray that you will bring revival to the land. I pray that you will provide your children with bread for this day. I pray that you will forgive us for our sins, conscious and unconscious. I pray that you will teach us compassion so that we will learn to forgive as you have forgiven us. I pray that your hand will guide us on good paths and away from temptations and you will strengthen us so that we will resist all deceptions. I pray this because you are God. To you be all glory and power forever. Amen.*

My eyes will be on the faithful in the land, that they may
dwell with me; he whose walk is blameless will minister to me.
No one who practices deceit will dwell in my house;
no one who speaks falsely will stand in my presence.

—PSALM 101:6–7

KNOWING GOD

WHAT DOES GENUINE faith look like? Can it be associated with advanced degrees in theology? Perhaps. Can faith be perceived through moving oratory? Maybe. Or can faith be found in someone who does good works day in and day out? I think that is very possible.

But all of these things—theology, oratory, and works—are not the source but are rather the out-workings from the source. The source for Christians is belief in the truthfulness of the evidence contained in the New Testament. Christ's words and the words of his witnesses serve as a window through which we can answer Jesus' question to his disciples: "But who do you say that I am?" (Matthew 16:15).

Faith for Christians is faith in the Lordship of Jesus Christ. In His own time and in ours, the world seems to believe in almost anything but Jesus Christ. So faith in Christ asks us to be strong and courageous, for we can anticipate being disregarded, confronted, and scorned, but that should never be a surprise. Even many of Jesus' own disciples became discouraged and abandoned Him (John 6:66).

The world provides many things for us to believe in, but God provided His Son, Jesus Christ, only once. He did His part. Now it is up to us. Will we believe or shall we put our faith and our trust in something or someone else? The Gospels serve as the best way to answer Jesus' question to his own disciples: "But who do you say that I am?"

Do not put your trust in princes, in mortal men,

who cannot save. When their spirit departs, they return to the

ground; on that very day their plans come to nothing.

—PSALM 146:3–4

TO BELIEVE

WHAT DO YOU really believe in? Some will say they do not believe in anything, but even in this case, the statement is a belief in non-belief. The issue is not so much about the existence of belief as an essential characteristic of all human beings; rather, it comes down to the foundational truth underlying our beliefs. Institutions are full of people who have strong beliefs, but in these instances, the believer's faith is often deeply singular and unconnected to a greater truth.

Some believe in the saving power of education or intelligence or of the goodness of government programs or their own physical prowess. But biblical wisdom warns us away, not from faith, but faith in something that cannot save. Stop a moment and ask: "What is my deepest belief?" If I have to choose to stake my life on something, where do I draw the line in the sand?

In the end, we walk on a path marked by our beliefs. If the belief that propels our life forward is unconnected to truth, then how will it lead to a place that in the end will prove to be good for us and for those who have known us.

The stone the builders rejected has become the capstone;

the LORD has done this, and it is marvelous in our eyes.

This is the day the LORD has made;

let us rejoice and be glad in it.

—PSALM 118:22–24

A NEW DAY

HOW WE ENTER a new day is generally how we will experience the entire day. For over twenty-eight years I have begun the day by reading and reflecting on the passages provided in the "Daily Service," a two-year lectionary found toward the back of the *Book of Common Prayer.*

Jonathan Aitken had reached the pinnacle of a political career in Great Britain that put him in contention to become the next prime minister. Then his world fell apart; he was arrested for various crimes and he found himself in a jail cell with the lowest of the low. He had fallen from the top to the bottom, losing everything, but in the midst of his despair, he discovered the Bible, and soon enough discovered a lectionary that put him in touch with the Word of God for the first time in his life.

In an article on "the Lectionary Life," Aitken quotes Thomas Cranmer from the 1662 *Book of Common Prayer*: "Blessed Lord who has caused all holy scripture to be written for our learning: Grant that we may in such wise hear them, read, mark, learn, and inwardly digest them…"

Aitken goes on to say, "the point of the lectionary is that it guides readers through well-trodden paths of Scripture with unseen companions, conservatively numbered in the hundreds of millions, from all parts of the body of Christ around the world."

This is exactly what happened in my own life; on February 13th, 1991, I joined millions of Christians on a journey of joy in discovering daily that indeed "all Scripture is breathed out by God and (is) profitable for teaching, for reproof, for correction, and for training in righteousness." (2 Timothy 3:18). I had entered not only a new day; I had discovered, along with Jonathan Aitken and millions of others, a new world and a pathway to a better one.

Then I realized that it is good and proper for a man to eat and drink, and to find satisfaction in his toilsome labor under the sun during the few days of life God has given him—for this is his lot. Moreover, when God gives any man wealth and possessions, and enables him to enjoy them, to accept his lot and be happy in his work—this is a gift of God. He seldom reflects on the days of his life, because God keeps him occupied with gladness of heart.

—ECCLESIASTES 5:18–20

A DEFINING MOMENT

THE DAY WAS Ash Wednesday, February 13, 1991. My family and I were on an island in the Caribbean, which was not a well-traveled place because the U.S. Navy had reserved large sections of the island for practice bombing runs. The bombs were no longer falling, and the house we were renting was situated near the top of a hill, providing panoramic views of the Atlantic and Caribbean oceans. It was in that house on that day that I unexpectedly came across a two-year lectionary hidden deep in the pages of the *Book of Common Prayer*. When I discovered this lectionary, it was if I heard a voice telling me that this was exactly what I needed as a way to come to know the whole Bible. So on that day many years ago, I quietly committed myself to following this biblical road map every day of the year no matter where I was or what I was doing.

And thus began my response to God's call. I would honor God by coming to know His Word by setting aside time every morning of every day. This journey would be slow, and it would require perseverance. But if I was going to truly honor God with my life, I would have to be equipped with a deeper understanding of God's Word. And through an everyday encounter with the Old and New Testaments, I began to understand what it meant to walk on God's ancient pathways.

CITY OF MAN

When I consider your heavens, the work of your fingers,

the moon and the stars, which you have set in place, what is

man that you are mindful of him, the son of man that you care

for him? You made him a little lower than the heavenly beings

and crowned him with glory and honor.

—PSALM 8:3–5

THE HOPELESSNESS OF MAN WITHOUT GOD

WHAT IS MAN apart from God? If we look at recent history, we see a creature that, through his behavior, more accurately reflects the frightening monsters of horror films than the being described here as "made a little lower than the heavenly beings and crowned . . . with glory and honor."

The long, sorry history of mankind wandering in the wilderness of godlessness is perfectly summarized in the first chapter of Paul's letter to the Romans. It is a tough minded picture, but it is hard to deny the truth of what Paul is saying: "Since they did not think it worthwhile to retain the knowledge of God, he gave them over to a depraved mind, to do what ought not to be done. They have become filled with every kind of wickedness, evil, greed and depravity. They are full of envy, murder, strife, deceit and malice. They are gossips, slanderers, God-haters, insolent, arrogant and boastful; they invent ways of doing evil; they disobey their parents; they are senseless, faithless, heartless, ruthless. Although they know God's righteous decree that those who do such things deserve death, they not only continue to do these very things but also approve of those who practice them" (Romans 1:28–32).

Man apart from God is profoundly prone to corruption. Paul paints an unvarnished picture of what men and women really look like when they choose to live without God. It is a choice, but the good news is that our story does not have to end that way. God has provided a way, through the cross of Jesus Christ, that can transform the condition of the worst of us into saints who are "crowned . . . with glory and honor."

A wise king winnows out the wicked;
he drives the threshing wheel over them.
The lamp of the LORD searches the spirit of a man;
it searches out his inmost being.
Love and faithfulness keep a king safe;
through love his throne is made secure.
The glory of young men is their strength,
gray hair the splendor of the old.

—PROVERBS 20:26–29

EVERYTHING IS PERMITTED

IN THE NINETEENTH century, many members of the intelligentsia decided that the God of the Bible was false and irrelevant. Whether it was through the work of Darwin, Marx, or Nietzsche, God, for the most part, was ushered off the stage. This created a new problem: Who would lead the way in establishing the new world order? If mankind were to continue to climb to ever-higher levels of technological and scientific achievement, then a substitute standard and standard bearer would be required. It was Nietzsche who proposed the idea of the Overlord or Ubermensch.

Another nineteenth-century writer, Fyodor Dostoyevsky, saw a darker side to the "God Is Dead" movement. He wrote in *The Brothers Karamazov*, "If God does not exist, then everything is permitted." It would not be until the twentieth century that the world would be able to test the practical applications underpinning the godless Overlord. And by then it was too late. The hope of the nineteenth century devolved into the horrific political and scientific perversions of the twentieth. It turns out that, when everything is permitted, "everything" inevitably includes Nazi death camps and Soviet Gulags. In the hands of the dictatorial Ubermensch, whether Hitler or Stalin or Mao, the people would be liberated into a demonic level of suffering.

For in his own eyes he flatters himself too
much to detect or hate his sin.

—PSALM 36:2

FROM HEAVENLY TO HELLISH

WHEN EVIL IMPULSES are incubating deep within the human heart, it is often hard for us, as well as others, to detect it. The Psalmist says we flatter ourselves and become experts at self-justification. And as we become consumed by the evil desires within, outwardly we engage in lies and deceit. The progress of wickedness is often slow and plodding at first, but with time it consumes the whole person, toppling the entire edifice.

In his book, *Mere Christianity*, C. S. Lewis wrote, "Every time you make a choice you are turning the central part of you, the part that chooses, into something a little different from what it was before. And taking your life as a whole, with all your innumerable choices, all your life long you are slowly turning this central thing either into a heavenly creature or into a hellish creature; either a creature that is in harmony with God, and with other creatures, and with itself, or else into one that is in a state of war and hatred with God, and with its fellow creatures and with itself. To be the one kind of creature is heaven; that is, it is joy and peace and knowledge and power. To be the other means madness, horror, idiocy, rage, impotence, and eternal loneliness. Each of us at each moment is progressing to the one state or the other."

A word was secretly brought to me, my ears caught
a whisper of it. Amid disquieting dreams in the night,
when deep sleep falls on men, fear and trembling seized
me and made all my bones shake.

—JOB 4:12–14

A DESCENT INTO HELL

LISTEN TO WHAT Eliphaz, a friend of Job, is saying: "Amid disquieting dreams in the night . . . a spirit glided past my face. . . . A form stood before my eyes and I heard a hushed voice" (Job 4:15,16). He is filled with fear, making his bones shake. Eliphaz came face to face with spiritual reality, which reminded me of Howard Storm and his story as it is recounted in his bestselling book, *My Descent into Death: A Second Chance at Life.*

One summer day in Paris in the mid-1980s, Howard Storm became violently ill and was taken to a hospital where he appeared to die. He tells of rising from his own body and looking around the room and hearing voices beckoning him to follow. He is persuaded to leave the hospital room but begins to feel a desire to turn back. However, the voices become insistent, then vicious, and finally violent. They start devouring him, but deep within he has enough strength to call out in desperation to Jesus with a prayer, begging for help. Suddenly, light appears, and Howard returns to his bed and life.

Howard began that hot summer day as an atheist; he emerged shaken and changed forever. The modern mind refuses to consider the reality of both heaven and hell, but Howard's compelling story of death and miraculous rebirth should prompt the skeptics to reconsider their assumptions.

It is better to take refuge in the LORD than to trust in man.
It is better to take refuge in the LORD than to trust in princes.

—PSALM 118:8–9

ACCEPT NO SUBSTITUTES

THE TEMPTATION TO create our own gods is almost irresistible. And once we have landed on the god of our choice, we move immediately to worship, casting aside reason and experience in our rush to laud the object of our desire. The object could be anything: a baseball team or a woman. It could be a Hollywood star or a politician. We seem to need to manufacture something or someone who is greater than we are, and so we put our trust in man and in princes even though the evidence would suggest that neither men nor princes are very trustworthy.

The tendency to worship mortals is like accepting the counterfeit for the original. The author of Hebrews addresses this human foible when he says that what we have here is "a copy and shadow of what is in heaven" (Hebrews 8:5). Jesus' claim is that He is the original and not a mere copy. While the world is always attempting to discredit and downgrade Him, Jesus keeps reminding us that He is the authentic one who can always be counted on.

Jesus said that others would come in His name (Matthew 24:5) and "many false prophets will appear and deceive many people" (Matthew 24:11), and all this has come true, especially in our own time; but Jesus continues to shine through all the darkness and confusion as the One, the only one we can trust.

Confuse the wicked, O Lord, confound their speech, for I see
violence and strife in the city. Day and night they prowl about
on its walls; malice and abuse are within it. Destructive forces
are at work in the city; threats and lies never leave its streets.

—PSALM 55:9–11

CITIZENS OF THE CITY

LONG BEFORE JERUSALEM fell to invaders, corruption had undermined the strength of its foundations. Jerusalem had been built as a place to honor and praise God; it was a citadel of peace, a place that protected the innocent and weak and promoted justice and godliness. Yet when the leaders of the city forgot God and began to honor only themselves, then "malice and abuse" began to roam within its walls; then the destructive forces of "violence and strife" came out of hiding, and "threats and lies" replaced truth and righteousness.

This persistent pattern of man betraying his Creator can be traced back to the biblical account of the cities of the plains: "The outcry against Sodom and Gomorrah is so great and their sin so grievous that I will go down and see if what they have done is as bad as the outcry that has reached me" (Genesis 18:20–21).

Sadly, what he found was worse, and even though he would have shown mercy if a few righteous men were found there, He found an utterly godless place where all "are corrupt and their ways are vile; there is no one who does good" (Psalm 53:1).

When men fall into full rebellion against God through sin, then the consequences are predictable; only the timing is not. As citizens of the city, we should always remember the pattern of drift and decline and turn back to God in all haste: "Put on sackcloth, O priests, and mourn; wail you who minister before the altar. . . . For the day of the LORD is near; it will come like destruction from the Almighty" (Joel 1:13, 15).

Do not be quick with your mouth,

do not be hasty in your heart to utter anything before God.

God is in heaven and you are on earth, so let your words be few.

As a dream comes when there are many cares,

so the speech of a fool when there are many words.

—ECCLESIASTES 5:2–3

KEEPING GOD OUT

IN MY FIRST year in college, I took an anthropology class that attempted to provide a comprehensive definition of man as distinct from all the other species on the earth. I remember reading of several definitions such as "tool maker," but the one that seemed to work the best was the concept that man was a "word maker."

Since this was a science class, no one pointed out that the Bible supported this idea—except for causation. For in the Bible, the Word first comes from God: "In the beginning was the Word, and the Word was with God, and the Word was God" (John 1:1). So when God created man in His own image, He gave man the gift of the word as well as the responsibility to name the creatures of the earth (Genesis 2: 19–20).

My science class arrived at the right definition of man; they just left out the reason why the Word is central to our human nature. The mystery of the origin of the Word was beyond the scope of this science class because it was assumed that all causation could only rise out of the forces in the natural world. It would be considered scientific heresy to suggest that the Word originated before nature.

C.S. Lewis says, "Does the whole vast structure of modern naturalism depend not on positive evidence but simply on an *a priori* metaphysical prejudice? Was it devised not to get in facts but to keep out God?"

Teach us to number our days aright,
that we may gain a heart of wisdom.

—PSALM 90:12

THE INCLINATIONS OF THE HEART

IN OUR OWN times, wisdom has been relocated from the heart to the head. This is based on the idea that an accumulation of information will somehow lead to wisdom if we can just sort through the mass of facts and figures free-floating through our daily lives. But are we right to somehow link "knowing" to wisdom?

David Mamet sees right through the "knowledge conceit" when he points out that to maintain illogical belief systems, the believers themselves "have to pretend not to know a lot of things."

Adam and Eve changed the very nature of the love of God in their hearts when they fell for the promise that they "will be like God, knowing good and evil" if only they would eat of the fruit of that tree (Genesis 3:5). It was that tragic act that turned the human heart away from the fullness of the love of God to darker inclinations. By the time of Noah, the infection of the heart had become so severe that God decided to "blot out man who I created from the face of the earth....The Lord saw that the wickedness of man was great in the earth, and that every inclination of the thoughts of the heart was only evil continually" (Genesis 6:5-6).

After the fall in the Garden, the human heart became overwhelmed with conflicting inclinations. The heart's natural love of God became corrupted by competing loves that drove out our primary love. Wisdom comes through a deep preference to love God first above everything else, even if that love causes the world to place itself (in small and large ways) in opposition to a believer in Christ. Jesus came into the world to transform the corrupted inclinations of our hearts by restoring the desire "to love the Lord your God with all your heart and with all your soul and with all your mind" (Matthew 22:37).

The highway of the upright avoids evil; he who guards his way
guards his life. Pride goes before destruction, a haughty spirit
before a fall . . . There is a way that seems right to a man,
but in the end it leads to death.

—PROVERBS 16:17–18,25

IN EVERY CORNER OF THE WORLD

A FATHER OFTEN will express pride in his son or daughter and a worker will be proud of a task well done, but this is not the pride of "a haughty spirit," nor is it the pride that "goes before destruction." The seeds of the pride that kills can be found in the earliest chapters of Genesis where the serpent persuades Eve to defy God's warning not to eat of the tree of the knowledge of good and evil. The serpent tells her that if she eats of this tree, she "will be like God" (Genesis 3:5). Both Adam and Eve make themselves number one by defying God. By wanting to be like God, they deny their own human nature as created by God and fall into the self-consciousness of self-love.

The pattern was set at the very beginning of human history: with man's disastrous tendency to deny God by exalting self. The so-called agnostics may not be certain about the existence of God, but they surely put a huge emphasis on themselves. They repeat the self-destructive mistake of our earliest ancestors.

When you defy God, you deny God and thereby make yourself into a false god to fill the void. It is hard to miss this, for evidence abounds on every street in every city in every corner of the world.

The eyes of the LORD are everywhere, keeping watch on
the wicked and the good. The tongue that brings healing is
a tree of life, but a deceitful tongue crushes the spirit. . . .
The house of the righteous contains great treasure,
but the income of the wicked brings them trouble.

—PROVERBS 15:3–4, 6

HIGH-TECH PROPHETS

IN THE EARLY days of the "Internet Revolution," many of the high-tech prophets sold the world on the transformative power of this new form of communication. Dot-com wizards, hardly out of their teens, became instant paper millionaires, and the world gazed in wonder on this new phenomenon. There was only one problem— the Internet was created by people.

Soon a common medical term became an ominous threat to all users of the Internet. Viruses started invading computers and computer networks. New businesses had to be built to fortify systems against alien invasions, and so the battle began.

We should not be surprised. The computer virus is really no different than a person becoming infected by sin. Everything is working according to plan when suddenly the system begins to demonstrate strange and uncharacteristic behaviors. A virus slips through the defenses, and our behavior begins to malfunction. We begin to lie or stir up dissension or stop working and start squandering our wealth and our gifts.

As Paul explains it, "I do not understand what I do. For what I want to do I do not do, but what I hate I do" (Romans 7:15). Once again, technology becomes the instrument of our human nature— including the darker side of it.

Remember your Creator in the days of your youth, before the
days of trouble come and the years approach when you will say,
"I find no pleasure in them". . . when the doors to the street are
closed and the sound of grinding fades; when men rise up at the
sound of birds, but all their songs grow faint; when men are
afraid of heights and of dangers in the streets; when the almond
tree blossoms and the grasshopper drags himself along and desire
no longer is stirred. Then man goes to his eternal home and
mourners go about the streets.

—ECCLESIASTES 12:1,4–5

THE OLD MAN AT THE WINDOW

THOUSANDS OF YEARS have passed since Solomon wrote this description of old age, but there is nothing old about it. It is immediate and contemporary, and we can see and feel the dusty street "where the grasshopper drags himself along." Even if we are young, we can imagine, through this verse, what old age feels like.

The poet transports us back in time to an old man, and there we are, sitting in the shaded room by that same window, unable to hear the sounds of children playing in the street or the music of the organ grinder. It is not hard to imagine that old man was once like one of the little children playing in the street outside of the window. And one day at some point in the future the child playing outside the window will one day become the old man who looks out at the world where "songs grow faint."

To you I call, O Lᴏʀᴅ my Rock; do not turn a deaf ear to me.
For if you remain silent, I will be like those who have gone down
to the pit. Hear my cry for mercy as I call to you for help,
as I lift up my hands toward your Most Holy Place.

—PSALM 28:1–2

A LIGHT IN THE RUINS

Aɴ Aᴍᴇʀɪᴄᴀɴ ᴍɪssɪᴏɴᴀʀʏ who once lived in Ukraine told me a story about an encounter he had with a friendly atheist. This young woman was giving him a tour around the city of Odessa. As they walked from place to place, she began to open up, and at one point, she told him that believing in God was ridiculously irrational. How could any educated person believe that God existed? She was not belligerent; she just stated her belief as a proven fact. She indicated that she was doing fine without God in her life.

As they were talking, they came to a blighted intersection that was nothing more than a ruin left over from the devastation of World War II. The empty, decaying structures were fragmented shells. Rubble rather than trees created an impression of a wasteland. Even flowers and weeds seemed to avoid this desolate place.

It was at that moment that my missionary friend turned to the woman and observed: "Look around. If you want to know what the world looks like without God, here it is right before us." She gazed at the wretched scene and seemed to make the link between a war-torn world and mankind's banishment of God from this modern and enlightened world. Did she see the relationship between famine, disease, and war, and our fractured relationship with the God who created us and nurtured us? Can love even exist in such a place? My missionary friend believes he touched her by using that desolate scene as a way of introducing God back into her life. He did not make his point with words or with arguments or talking points. He just revealed the obvious, and he let that do its work in her heart.

THE SOJOURNER

There are three things that are too amazing for me,
four that I do not understand: the way of an eagle in the sky,
the way of a snake on a rock, the way of a ship on the high seas,
and the way of a man with a maiden.

—PROVERBS 30:18–19

WINTER LIGHT

IN EARLY FEBRUARY the light begins to change. Without much warning, the steel gray of deep winter gives way to intimations of a softer season ahead. Daylight lingers longer into the afternoon, and the warmth of the light reflecting off distant skyscrapers seems to battle the forbidding coldness of the moment. And in the late afternoon, when the sky is clear, the setting sun paints the western horizon in orange and reds, intimating that the cloistered winter months will soon be past.

This is the time when I begin to feel the draw of the hills and mountains of the country beyond the shores of this water-bound city. Though snow and ice still cover much of the surrounding land, I instinctively begin to plan to head out to the territory of the Appalachian Mountains and the trail that connects the twelve states between Georgia and Maine.

I am often asked why I leave the comforts of home to walk the many miles of the Appalachian Trail, and I suppose I have many reasons, but what I always come back to is the way the trail connects me to the mysteries of this life we have all fallen into. I may inhabit a world constructed by the hands of man, and I may marvel at all its complexity and brilliance, but the city of man with its activities and diversions is never enough.

Solomon attributes this longing to the way God made men and women, for while we live in the temporal, we yearn for things eternal (Ecclesiastes 3:11). When the Psalmist says, "The meadows are covered with flocks and the valleys are mantled with grain; they shout for joy and sing" (Psalm 65:13), he sees the loving handprint of God in everything. So even though my feet are planted firmly on the hard ground of this world, my heart tells me that eternal inclinations buried deep within my soul urge me on to walk where "the hills are clothed with gladness" (Psalm 65:12).

Have you journeyed to the springs of the sea or walked in the
recesses of the deep? Have the gates of death been shown to you?
Have you seen the gates of the shadow of death? Have you
comprehended the vast expanses of the earth?
Tell me, if you know all this.

—JOB 38:16–18

A SHIPWRECK

IN HIS INTRODUCTION to G. K. Chesterton's *Orthodoxy*, Philip
Yancey writes that the world we live in is "a sort of cosmic shipwreck.
A person's search for meaning resembles a sailor who awakens
from a deep sleep and discovers treasure strewn about, relics from
a civilization he can barely remember. One by one he picks up the
relics . . . and tries to discern their meaning." He goes on to compare
the scattered remnants washed ashore from a shipwreck to "bits of
Paradise extended through time."

When I am out hiking, I find it easier to see myself as just another
restless wanderer of the earth. I walk through unfamiliar landscapes,
up one side of a mountain and down the other where my identity
is not defined by job or education or home. I am stripped of these
layers of identity. I am liberated to see the world through a more
poetic imagination, marveling at the mystery and beauty of what I
am encountering.

Walking the ridges of the Presidential Range in New
Hampshire, I come across huge boulders, some the size of small
houses, lying scattered everywhere, with some resting precariously
at the edge of deep ravines. This vast, improbable, stone-strewn
landscape prompts all kinds of responses from a sense of natural
grandeur to how did this strange arrangement of rocks happen
in the first place? In the end I am left with a sense of the strange
improbability of it all. It is perhaps the Psalmist who understands
the mystery of creation best: "O Lord, how manifold are your
works! In wisdom have you made them all; the earth is full of

your creatures. Here is the sea, great and wide, which teems with creatures innumerable, living things both small and great. There go the ships, and Leviathan, which you formed to play in it." (Psalm 104: 24-26)

You, O Lord, keep my lamp burning;
my God turns my darkness into light.

—PSALM 18:28

ILLUMINATION

A RENOWNED LANDSCAPE photographer once told me, "I am just an average photographer with a very great God." I am an average photographer, but I know the truth of his observation through an experience of my own.

It began on an early spring climb to the summit of Mt. Whitney in the High Sierras. This climb was not the usual hike up to the summit, but a four-day adventure that required heavy backpacking up to snow-filled Boy Scout Lake, a flat bowl surrounded on three sides by sharp, jutting peaks. This natural platform was our base camp; from there, we ascended Whitney by heading up a long, steep, icy shoot to the right of the imposing headwall. About five hundred feet below the summit, we clamped onto fixed ropes for the final push.

After descending, we spent that night once again at Boy Scout Lake. The next morning, we awoke before sunrise to begin the job of packing up to head down to the Portal and the road out to Lone Pine. At higher elevations, the world before sunrise can be cold and miserable, but when the rising sun appeared and its ascending light hit the dormant gray rocks, the rocks seemed to awaken and catch fire and dance with the new dawn.

Just south of our tent site stand the Needles, four sculpted spires that rise up out of the mountain massif. They appear to the eye to be four steeples of a natural cathedral standing guard against the brutal wind that is constantly besieging this massive wall.

For the most part, I was busy packing up for our departure, but when I chanced to look up, I could see that the light had transformed the stone spires of the Needles into a luminous, serrated gold bulwark set against the deep blue of a desert morning sky. Luckily, my camera was resting on my sleeping bag; I picked it up and without hesitation, shot four or five frames with black and white film. I wanted to catch the gold rocks, but I had run out of color film, so I had no choice but to go with what was in the camera.

When I later developed the film, I could see that the gold that had caught my eye became, in the picture, vibrantly beautiful rock formations. I had caught the light as it reflected off the Needles in just the right way at just the right moment. If I had hesitated, the light would have changed, and my exceptional black and white picture would have lost all its life. Instead, I became a very average photographer recording the work of a very great God.

He makes springs pour water into the ravines;
it flows between the mountains. They give water to all the beasts
of the field; the wild donkeys quench their thirst. The birds of
the air nest by the waters; they sing among the branches.
He waters the mountains from his upper chambers;
the earth is satisfied by the fruit of his work.

—PSALM 104:10–13

MARCH MADNESS

IN THE SPRING of each year, hundreds, if not thousands, of enthusiastic hikers take their first steps on a 2,193-mile journey on the Appalachian Trail. Months of preparation have led to this moment. They have read guidebooks, bought equipment, packed food, and talked to those who have hiked before them. They have diligently studied every aspect of the journey to come, and now they stand under the stone portal as they prepare to ascend Springer Mountain, the true starting point of the trail.

Yet no amount of study can prepare these hikers for what lies ahead. Nature is beautiful and alluring and very hard. Hikers can expect sore knees, turned ankles, persistent thirst, lonely nights, and lingering doubts. They will be slowed by blizzards in the Smokies, startled by lightning strikes in Virginia, exhausted by searing summer heat in Pennsylvania, drenched by chilling downpours in New Hampshire, and tested by everything in Maine.

But as they walk the trail and become hardened by its challenges, hikers will experience a change of heart and mind. With time and miles, a veteran slowly emerges; the novice at Springer becomes the confident and knowledgeable Thru-Hiker who will keep on striving to achieve victory over every large and small adversity. The postcard landscape of the armchair hiker has given way to a deeper understanding of living outside of the normal comforts of civilized life. What began as toil and trouble has become something akin to joy.

The seasoned hiker overcomes through endurance and perseverance. He has encountered unexpected obstacles time and again, but he forges on because he has a defined purpose, an endgame that over time draws ever closer. And as he closes in on the last peak, the last big challenge, a new energy flows into and through his body as the final pinnacle finally comes into sight. He has reached the summit ... and tomorrow is another day.

Praise the Lord from the earth . . . lightning and hail,
snow and clouds, stormy winds that do his bidding,
you his mountains and all hills, fruit trees and all cedars. . . .
Let them praise the name of the Lord.

—PSALM 148:7–9, 13

FORECAST: SNOW ON FLOWERS

It was April in Tennessee, and in the valleys budding trees, emerging flowers, and fields blanketed in green all heralded the warmth and joy of spring. But up on the ridge of the Appalachian range, winter clutched the white and gray wooded landscape with a relentless grip.

Before setting out on my twenty-two mile day trip, I kept imagining the valley picture of a warm sunlit walk in the woods, but at the trailhead, all I could see were gray clouds moving ominously across the skies from west to east. The wind was cold and sustained. This was not what I expected.

I started out with the hope of covering about three miles each hour. This was possible because elevation gain and loss on this section of the trail was moderate. So if I could maintain this pace, I would be able to finish before 5 p.m. However, the game plan did not include 30 mph winds sweeping across the mountain ridges.

And the plan did not allow for blizzard conditions that worsened throughout the day. I had envisioned a clear path, but the snow came hurling at me from all angles; after three arduous hours, I had covered a disappointing seven miles with fifteen miles still to go. The terrain had become clothed in white.

Occasionally, a northbound hiker would emerge out of the whiteness. We would stop and trade information and then quickly go our separate ways because, without movement, the cold would begin to penetrate through the layers of gear. The real benefit of meeting other hikers was the path they left providing me for a time with a marked way forward through the accumulating snow.

Eventually though, the wind would erase any evidence of the hiker's existence. I had to be careful not to lose my way.

Just after nightfall, I arrived at Vandeventer Shelter, located about three thousand feet above Watauga Lake. A few hikers were inside their tents near the shelter, but they did not bother to emerge, nor did I bother to stick around. By then, the storm had relinquished its firm grip on the mountains. Occasionally, the full moon peered out from behind passing clouds. Lights flickered around the lake, giving me the strong desire to keep trekking toward the warmth and safety below. But I still had over four miles of steep downs before reaching my car.

So I journeyed forward toward my destination, even though getting there had been fraught with unexpected twists and turns. Snow, wind, and cold kept trying to divert or turn me but I persisted toward the destination I had set out for earlier that day when I had been surrounded with intimations of a quiet and gentle Spring ridge walk in the Appalachian mountains.

He draws up the drops of water, which distill as rain to the
streams; the clouds pour down their moisture and abundant
showers fall on mankind. Who can understand how he spreads
out the clouds, how he thunders from his pavilion? See how he
scatters his lightning about him, bathing the depths of the sea.
This is the way he governs the nations and provides food in
abundance. He fills his hands with lightning and commands it
to strike its mark. His thunder announces the coming storm;
even the cattle make known its approach.

—JOB 36:27–33

A FLEETING MOMENT

MANY YEARS AGO, during my first long hike on the Appalachian Trail in New Hampshire, I witnessed a fleeting moment of beauty that I have never forgotten. Late one day, after an easy ten miles of walking on mostly flat ground, I began to search for a place to rest for the night. About a mile or so beyond a small town, I happened upon a cabin about fifty yards off the trail. Inside, the uninviting shelter was cold and dark. I dropped my gear and settled in resigning myself to a night in the woods alone.

After a light dinner, I felt an urge to get away from the gloom of the shelter, and so I left it to take a walk toward an open field on a hillside that was surrounded by thick woods. As I approached the field, the light from the declining sun drew contrasting shadows against the bright yellows and greens of the long, uncut grass. It was a picture of tranquility, and I was glad to bask in it.

As I stood in the midst of this natural still-life, I became aware of three deer grazing above me on the hillside. They did not notice me, and so I quietly gazed on that scene of tranquil beauty. Time seemed to suspend itself: even the wind briefly stood still. Just as quickly, though, a soft breeze cut across the scene, and the deer lifted their heads in unison, sensing an intruder. They hesitated a moment and then vanished into the shadows of the surrounding woods. Once again, I was in what had been a bright place; now, though, dusk was transforming the soft summer scene into something more ominous as the waning colors of the fields turned gray.

Now, all these years later, I remember that scene as if it were an image painted by God Himself. I felt the warmth of God's peace that day, but I had to turn back to the cold embrace of the lonely cabin. I did not know then that the journey ahead would often be long and hard. Yet, wherever life would lead me, I carried with me that image of momentary grace as sustenance for the journey ahead, regardless of the conditions, whether easy or difficult.

Oh, for the days when I was in my prime,
when God's intimate friendship blessed my house.

—JOB 29:4

───⊙∞⊙───

INTIMACY

THE THING TO remember about Eden is that it was an intimate place. There was no division between God, the Creator, and man, the creature He created. There was no division between the man and the woman; they lived intimately. And the first man and first woman were one with their environment. It was the perfect place for them to worship God and enjoy His blessings. But paradise was lost, and when that happened, mankind lost the intimacy that God created us for; we have yearned to recover ever since.

As a child, my own little corner of paradise was a lake in New Hampshire that I lived on every July for three years. When I think of that place, the memory in my heart takes me instantly back, and there I am on my cot in a small cabin on the lake's shore. Outside, moths and other insects, drawn by the light of my reading lamp, buzz against the screened windows. I can smell the scent of pine that permeates the soft summer evening air. And behind the nocturnal sounds of crickets and frogs, I hear the rhythmic lapping of gentle waves as they softly touch the rocks near where I am resting my head.

And I remember how, early in the morning, my father would invite his boys to join him on a walk up Bean road to a small local farm. As we walked along the road, we could feel a mountain chill in the air, and we could see the mist suspended like a blanket above the green fields. The farm itself rested between the road and the lower reaches of Red Hill, and so we gathered up some strawberries or raspberries and thick heavy cream to take back to our cottage for the family breakfast.

Of course, in this idealized setting, I suffered the normal worldly intrusions of fights, skinned knees, hurt feelings, and the rest, but as I now think back to my time on that lake in New Hampshire, I am reminded that the intimacy I experienced there is but a shadow of the intimacy that God wants to experience with all of His children.

You have made known to me the path of life;
you will fill me with joy in your presence,
with eternal pleasures at your right hand.

—PSALM 16:11

EXPOSED

ONCE IN A while it is a good thing to be reminded of one's own vulnerability. Not that we should risk danger unnecessarily, but neither should we pretend that we can permanently insulate ourselves from the tempest and the storm. For "man is born to trouble" (Job 5:7), and to try to live a bubble existence outside the perimeter of that reality is to stake one's life on the premise that trouble will never knock at our own door.

One early spring day, I set out on the Appalachian Trail in southwestern Virginia. I planned to cover 56 miles over three days; I packed under the assumption that I would spend each night in a shelter, which meant I would not need to carry the extra weight of a tent. After a late start and many miles of relatively flat walking, I reached the base of Chestnut Knob, a 4,400-foot peak with an open summit ridge.

I ascended without much difficulty, but the weather deteriorated as I approached the long ridge. Strong winds and rain swirled around me. I quickly changed into rain gear and set out for the shelter still 2.5 miles ahead. I walked as fast as I could because time suddenly was not on my side; dusk was setting in, turning the open, wet landscape into a lonely and somewhat forbidding place. Soon I reached some woods where the path seemed to begin to descend. I checked the guidebook, which suggested the warden's shelter was near the summit. Suddenly doubt entered my mind: Could I have walked past the shelter in my rush to get there?

Soon the gray of dusk became the darkness of night. If I turned back to hunt for the shelter on the exposed ridge, I could easily lose the trail. And if I had missed the shelter, pushing ahead would have left me no better off. My expectations of sleeping in a dry shelter quickly evaporated. I was without my tent; I had lost my bearings, and I needed to make a decision. Experience and intuition told me to stay put until the morning. And that is what I did. I placed my sleeping bag on the wet ground, got in, and tried to fall asleep. I worried throughout the night that the rain would soak through my bag, but for the most part the bag stayed dry on the inside. Still, the wind did not relent, often sounding like an advancing freight train as it slammed into the western side of the ridge. But eventually morning broke, and I emerged to resume my trek north.

Sometimes our choices are reduced to what is the least bad thing to do. That night, I lost the usual comforts that can often dull our awareness of the nature of the world we live in. Sometimes, our one option is to stay put. And that is what I did. The night was lonely, wet and uncomfortable and it once again reminded me of the thin line between danger and well-being.

My eyes are dim with grief. I call to you, O LORD, every day;
I spread out my hands to you . . . But I cry to you for help,
O LORD; in the morning my prayer comes before you.

—PSALM 88:9, 13

TRAIL ANGELS

ARTHUR, MY SIXTEEN-YEAR-OLD son, and I were fifteen miles into an eighteen-mile day on the Appalachian Trail in Pennsylvania. We started early that morning in the small river town of Duncannon. We crossed the Susquehanna on a well-travelled bridge, ascended a moderate ridge, and then began the long, rocky trek north. The temperature was mild for August, but the long miles began to wear us down.

A few days before we started out on this journey, I had arranged to have a "trail angel" pick us up at an isolated road crossing in an isolated section of state forestland, as we would need a ride back to Duncannon when we finished. But as the miles passed by and it became time to call to connect with our ride, the phone failed. The day was drawing to a close, and my heart began to sink as we descended toward the road crossing.

Would we have to spend an uncomfortable night in the woods, or worse, would we be forced to walk back? It is in moments like this that we realize the extent of our own vulnerability. We were completely dependent on the good will of strangers. But as we approached the road, I began to hear voices. Like a guardian angel, the stranger and his wife had kept their appointment. Just as the cloud of anxiety had dominated my mood for a number of miles, now with the knowledge that we were saved from a variety of unpleasant outcomes, a wave of gratitude and joy flooded into my heart. At that moment, I felt a small touch of God's goodness, and I could say with all my heart that Arthur and I were blessed by the goodness of two "Trail Angels."

I lift my hands to you in prayer.
I thirst for you as parched land thirsts for rain.

—PSALM 143:6

GENUINE THIRST

I WAS HIKING in the Selway-Bitterroot Wilderness in Montana when I took a wrong turn. I thought I was on the right track, and I was comforted by the fact that the map showed a small body of water up ahead, so I continued on.

But as I climbed higher, the land grew drier; trees and vegetation gave way to dust and unrelenting heat, and my supply of water quickly dwindled to a few drops. I thought of turning back, but I foolishly made the decision to forge ahead to what became even drier and more isolated ground.

Within an hour, the water shown on the map became a longing, then an obsession, then an urgent necessity. With every step I was becoming more desperate. Then just when my hope was turning to despair, I stumbled upon a shallow pool of still water. Without hesitation, I drank it as if it were the sweetest water I had ever tasted. I experienced overwhelming relief and joy at something as common as water because my body desperately needed replenishment.

What is true for the body depleted of life-giving water is just as true for the soul of any person wandering in a spiritual wasteland. David says, "As a deer pants for streams of water, so my soul pants for you, O God. My soul thirsts for God, for the living God" (Psalm 42:1–2). And elsewhere, he says, "O God, you are my God, earnestly I seek you; my soul thirsts for you, my body longs for you, in a dry and weary land where there is no water" (Psalm 63:1).

Our physical nature mirrors a thirst dwelling deep within our heart. Will we find drink to quench this spiritual thirst, or will we continue farther into the dry land where there is no water to be found?

There is a way that seems right to a man,

but in the end it leads to death.

—PROVERBS 14:12

WHITE BLAZES

DON AND I had a late start the night before. Touches of winter were in the air even though we were only in the first week of October. By the time we reached Baldpate Shelter, it was night. Others were there preparing for bed, and soon, we too were in our sleeping bags.

The trail in Maine is rough; it is often wet, steep, and rocky. And the hiker also needs to stay alert for moose who occasionally use the trail as a pathway as they forage for food. Around noon, Don and I reached the summit of Baldpate; we spent about an hour there appreciating the fall landscape far below.

From there we descended sharply into Frye Notch. We stopped at a lean-to for a quick lunch and water refill. Don went to fill up his water bottle first; then, as I started to walk down to the stream, he pushed off to ascend Surplus Mountain. I was more concerned about water and paid no attention to Don leaving. But after I packed up, I noticed that two trails departed north from the shelter and neither had any markings. I looked at my map, but it gave no indication that two trails existed.

The Appalachian Trail is well known for its white blazes. Usually these markers are painted on trees every few hundred feet. They are essential for the hiker because often several trails can converge. Without a blaze or some kind of marker, the hiker would be reduced to guessing what way was the right way.

I had no idea which way Don had gone. If I chose the wrong way, I would be heading away from him. Or perhaps he chose the wrong path. If I was wrong, would he continue ahead or come back? Phones did not work, so it was possible that we would end up spending many frustrating hours trying to find each other.

I became troubled because I had to make a choice, which could easily be wrong. I started up the trail to the right, as it seemed more worn. As I ascended, I cried out several times only to be answered by the still silence of the Maine woods. Where are the blazes? Where is Don? Is he up ahead or back at the shelter? Suddenly, I doubted the rightness of every step. I felt lost, and I was angry that I had briefly let my guard down back at the shelter.

Jeremiah 6:16 says, "Stand at the crossroads and look. . ." Almost every day brings us to one or more crossroads. I was careless that October day in the woods of Maine, and I almost took the wrong way. As it turned out, I had made the right decision. Don was at the summit of Surplus Mountain. My worries dissipated, and we moved on to the next challenge.

*Two are better than one, because they have a good return
for their work: If one falls down, his friend can help him up.
But pity the man who falls and has no one to help him up! . . .
A cord of three strands is not quickly broken.*

—ECCLESIASTES 4:9–10, 12

A WALK IN THE WOODS

I ENJOY HIKING in the woods alone. On one particular trip, the trail took me up to a ridge on a low-lying mountain range in central Pennsylvania. On such trips, the familiar noises of civilization can often be heard: the distant rumble of a passing freight train or the subtle hum of an interstate or just the low-grade sounds of distant activity filtering up to the trail.

But on this particular day everything was different, for as I moved further along the rocky path, I began to notice the absence of sound. The feeling of isolation became palpable, and the sense of sudden vulnerability crept into my thoughts.

It is at times like this that one can feel a deep appreciation for the power of two. If I had fallen while alone, I would have been in trouble, but if a companion had been with me, I would have been helped. If I had become lost, my friend would have assisted in finding the way back to the trail. Alone, my chances of success would have been greatly diminished.

This noiseless world, beautiful and intriguing as it was, left me with a feeling of aloneness and mild foreboding. Quite suddenly, a bunch of "what ifs" flooded into my thinking and it seemed like I had stumbled into a world outside of God's design. I strongly felt the need for a companion. So while the walk was memorable, I was relieved, in the end, to hear all the familiar sounds of human activity once again. For to me these noises were the sound of friendship and safety. It even occurred to me that the noises from below were the sounds of love. It felt good to be back.

God is our refuge and strength, an ever-present help in trouble.
Therefore we will not fear, though the earth give way and the
mountains fall into the heart of the sea, though its waters roar
and foam and the mountains quake with their surging.

—PSALM 46:1–3

PURIFIED

THE SHENANDOAH NATIONAL Park is part of a thin strip of the Blue Ridge Mountains located in central Virginia. This section of the Appalachian Trail is a welcome change for hikers because the ups and downs are moderate, and the trail is never very far from the Blue Ridge Parkway.

I hiked this section in May 2005. The first few days were easy; I kept the mileage to a tolerable ten miles or so, finishing well before nightfall. But on the fourth day, I planned an eighteen-mile day in order to reach a cabin that the guidebook said provided a view east toward Old Rag Mountain and other lesser peaks. The temperature that day was fine for hiking, and the trail provided easy footing; but the climbs were more numerous than before, and I began to wear out.

The last big climb of the day was Bald Face Mountain, which by North Carolina and Tennessee standards was nothing special, but I had run low on energy, so I merely slogged along. When I was about halfway up the mountain, a bright idea dawned on me. Rather than suffer every miserable step, why not march up the rest of the way. I usually do not like to hike with music playing in my ears because I feel I will be missing part of the nature experience, but this time I put aside my concerns and began listening to Michael W. Smith's album, *Worship*.

I like many of Michael's songs, particularly "Above All," but as I neared the summit, his song "Purified" began to play. I don't know if you have ever heard it before, but it was the perfect song, for as I reached the summit, the amazing chorus reached a crescendo with the words, "I will stand in cleansing fire, by you I'm purified . . .

(for) you are Holy." Music and moment met together on that mountaintop, and for an instant, I felt as if I were walking on holy ground. I stopped to appreciate the view of the world all around me, and felt gratitude for the beauty and power of Michael W. Smith's song. Soon enough, though, the moment passed and I moved on in the twilight toward the cabin with a view.

Come, let us sing for joy to the LORD;

let us shout aloud to the Rock of our salvation.

Let us come before him with thanksgiving

and extol him with music and song.

—PSALM 95:1–2

SING AND MAKE MUSIC

As a boy, I found church intimidating. It didn't start out that way, because I had asked my parents if I could please go to church. They agreed, and one Sunday a church school bus picked me up and transported me and my older brother to a nearby church for worship and Sunday School. Even though I wanted to like the experience of attending church, I found it intimidating. Perhaps it was the building with its high arched ceilings, its long rows of half-empty pews, and its distant altar with larger-than-life wooden carvings of Jesus and His apostles. If the architect had envisioned "grand" as his primary consideration, then he succeeded heroically: Grand and cold. For a young boy with an attraction to Jesus, this particular place failed to create any sense of intimacy and joy. Instead, this church was a beautiful rendition of the historic church at a particular moment in time.

The Psalmist speaks of worship in terms of joy, thanksgiving, music, and song. Paul speaks of worship in terms of being filled with the Holy Spirit, of singing hymns and giving thanks to God for the immeasurable blessings of Jesus Christ (Ephesians 5:18–20).

The early church, as given to us in Scripture, had it right. It isn't about money or buildings or perfectly crafted sermons. It is about a passionate love and belief in our Lord and Savior Jesus Christ.

I lift up my eyes to the hills—where does my help come from?
My help comes from the LORD, the Maker of heaven and earth.

—PSALM 121:1–2

A FELLOW PASSENGER

I WAS ON an airplane heading for Nashville and, like almost everyone else, I was quietly minding my own business. But I did notice the lady sitting by the window on my aisle; she was looking out at the world beyond our cabin, and in her hands was a Bible. She was an older black woman, and she had a quiet strength and dignity about her.

Well into the two-hour flight, we began to talk about the usual superficial things, but I really wanted to talk to her about her Bible as I had begun reading Scripture myself a few years earlier. I don't remember many of the details of that conversation, but I was startled when she told me that she was a missionary from Africa who had come to the mission fields of the United States. Moreover, she told me that she often traveled from city to city without knowing where she would stay or whom she would help. Then she told me that the verse that she loved the most was Psalm 121:1: "I lift my eyes to the mountains—where does my help come from? My help comes from the LORD, the Maker of heaven and earth." As it turned out, that verse was one of my own favorites.

I treasure that simple encounter on an otherwise unremarkable airplane ride to Nashville. My preconceptions were knocked off balance when I was forced to realize that we need missionaries here in America just as much as Africa might need them. But it was not the mission that impressed me. It was the person sitting in that seat by the window, so meek and unassuming, so gentle and faithful. She clearly was one of God's children doing God's business in a way that would not attract much notice, but still, she had that unique concentrated power that has been changing the world quietly and effectively one person at a time for over two thousand years.

Praise the LORD. Praise the LORD from the heavens,
praise him in the heights above. Praise him, all his angels,
praise him, all his heavenly hosts. Praise him, sun and moon,
praise him, all you shining stars.

—PSALM 148:1–3

THE HEAVENS

HAVE YOU EVER ventured outside on a clear, cold, winter night and gazed into the heavens? Millions of tiny stars speckle the dark expanse, lighting up the world so that all can see the evidence of the glory, beauty, and majesty of the work of the Creator of all things.

Too many of us look up into the vast sparkling canvas of the universe and see only . . . nothingness. But when you look with the eyes of your heart on God, you see the handprint of the Divine. Thomas à Kempis sums this up in *Imitation of Christ*: "Therefore, I wish to offer and present to You the jubilant joy found in all devout hearts, their burning love, their ecstasies, their supernatural illuminations and heavenly visions, together with all the virtues and praises that have been or shall ever be given You by the creatures of heaven and earth, for myself and for all who have been recommended to my prayers and that You may receive fitting praise from men and be glorified without end."

POSTSCRIPT

A SHORT SELECTION OF FAVORITE VERSES

"A voice says, 'Cry!' And I said, 'What shall I cry?' All flesh is grass, and all its beauty is like the flower of the field. The grass withers, the flower fades when the breath of the Lord blows on it; surely the people are grass. The grass withers, the flower fades, but the word of our God will stand forever."

—ISAIAH 40:6-8

"Now the word of the LORD came to me, saying, 'Before I formed you in the womb I knew you, and before you were born I consecrated you; I appointed you a prophet to the nations.'"

—JEREMIAH 1:4-5

"Then he said to them, 'Go your way . . . . And do not be grieved, for the joy of the LORD is your strength.'"

—NEHEMIAH 8:10

"'And now, Israel, what does the LORD your God require of you, but to fear the LORD your God, to walk in all his ways, to love him, to serve the LORD with all your heart and with all your soul, and to keep the commandments and statutes of the LORD, which I am commanding you today for your good?'"

—DEUTERONOMY 10:12-13

"Thus says the LORD: 'Stand by the roads, and look, and ask for the ancient paths, where the good way is; and walk in it, and find rest for your souls. But they said, "We will not walk in it."'"

—JEREMIAH 6:16

"'The waters closed over me to take my life; the deep surrounded me; weeds were wrapped around my head at the roots of the mountains. I went down to the land whose bars closed upon me forever; yet you brought my life from the pit, O LORD my God. When my life was fainting away, I remembered the LORD, and my prayer came to you, into your holy temple.'"

—JONAH 2:5-7

"'Who is this that darkens counsel by words without knowledge? Where were you when I laid the foundation of the earth? Tell me, if you have understanding.Who determined its measurements-surely you know! Or who stretched the line upon it? On what were its bases sunk, or who laid its cornerstones, when the morning stars sang together and all the sons of God shouted for joy?'"

—JOB 38:2-7

"Where shall I go from your Spirit? Or where shall I flee from your presence? If I ascend to heaven, you are there! If I make my bed in Sheol, you are there! If I take the wings of the morning and dwell in the utmost parts of the sea, even there your hand will lead me, and your right hand shall hold me."
—Psalm 139:7-10

"How beautiful upon the mountains are the feet of him who brings good news, who publishes peace, who brings good news of happiness, who publishes salvation, who says to Zion, "'Your God reigns.'"

—ISAIAH 52:7

"'Therefore, I testify to you this day that I am innocent of the blood of all, for I did not shrink from declaring to you the whole counsel of God.'"

—ACTS 20:26

"'Therefore, O King Agrippa, I was not disobedient to the heavenly vision, but declared first to those in Damascus, then in Jerusalem, and throughout all the region of Judea, and also to the gentiles, that they should repent and turn to God, performing deeds in keeping with their repentance.'"

—ACTS 26:19-20

"To that end, keep alert with all perseverance, making supplication for all the saints, and also for me, that words may be given to me in opening my mouth boldly to proclaim the mystery of the gospel, for which I am an ambassador in chains, that I may declare it boldly, as I ought to speak."

—EPHESIANS 6:18-20

"'The God of Israel has spoken; the Rock of Israel has said to me; When one rules justly over men, ruling in the fear of God, he dawns on them like the morning light, like the sun shining forth on a cloudless morning, like rain that makes the grass to sprout from the earth.'"

—2 SAMUEL 23:2-4

"All of this is from God who through Christ reconciled us to himself and gave us the ministry of reconciliation; that is, in Christ God was reconciling the world to himself, not counting their trespasses against them, and entrusting to us the message of reconciliation. Therefore, we are ambassadors for Christ, God making his appeal through us. We implore you on behalf of Christ, be reconciled to God. For our sake he made him to be sin who had no sin, so that in him we might become the righteousness of God"

—2 CORINTHIANS 5:18-21